Contents

Any words appearing in the text in bold, **like this**, are explained in the Glossary.

What is a coral reef?

A coral reef is like a huge rock-garden under the sea. A reef is made of billions of tiny sea-animals called **corals**.

fish

coral

Corals look like brightly coloured plants growing in the water.

4

TAKE-OFF!

What are ...?
CORAL REEFS

Claire Llewellyn

Heinemann
LIBRARY

www.heinemann.co.uk
Visit our website to find out more information about Heinemann Library books.

To order:

 Phone 44 (0) 1865 888066

 Send a fax to 44 (0) 1865 314091

Visit the Heinemann Bookshop at www.heinemann.co.uk to browse our catalogue and order online.

First published in Great Britain by Heinemann Library,
Halley Court, Jordan Hill, Oxford OX2 8EJ,
a division of Reed Educational and Professional Publishing Ltd.
Heinemann is a registered trademark of Reed Educational and Professional Publishing Ltd.

OXFORD MELBOURNE AUCKLAND
JOHANNESBURG BLANTYRE GABORONE
IBADAN PORTSMOUTH (NH) USA CHICAGO

© Reed Educational and Professional Publishing Ltd 2001

The moral right of the proprietor has been asserted.

Designed by David Oakley
Illustrated by Hardlines and Jo Brooker
Originated by Dot Gradations
Printed by South China Printing in Hong Kong/China

ISBN 0 431 02442 1 (hardback)   ISBN 0 431 02447 2 (paperback)
05 04 03 02 01   05 04 03 02 01
10 9 8 7 6 5 4 3 2 1   10 9 8 7 6 5 4 3 2 1

British Library Cataloguing in Publication Data

Llewellyn, Claire
    What are coral reefs?. – (Take-off!)
    1.Coral reefs and islands – Juvenile literature 2.Coral reef ecology – Juvenile literature
    I.Title II.Coral reefs
    578.7'789

Acknowledgements
The publishers would like to thank the following for permission to reproduce photographs: Bruce Coleman: Timothy O'Keefe p.20, Larry Lipsky p.29; FLPA: G Lebois p.5, Ian Cartwright p.7, Silvestris p.8, David B Fleetham p.10; NASA: Johnson Space Centre p.22, p.24, p.26; Oxford Scientific Films: David B Fleetham p.6, p.16, Mark Webster p.14, Laurence Gould p.18; Robert Harding Picture Library: p.21; Still Pictures: Fred Bavendam p.4, Gerard & Margi Moss p.9, p.11, p.13, Truchet-Unep p.12, Yves Lefevre p.15, Norbert Wu p.17, Alberto Garcias/Christian Aid p.19, Roland Seitre p.28.

Cover photograph reproduced with permission of Still Pictures/Fred Bavendam.

Our thanks to Sue Graves and Hilda Reed for their advice and expertise in the preparation of this book.

Every effort has been made to contact copyright holders of any material reproduced in this book. Any omissions will be rectified in subsequent printings if notice is given to the publishers.

coral reef

shallow water

A coral reef looks like rocks under the water.

Most coral reefs are found in sunny, shallow waters in the warmest parts of the world.

Corals thrive in warm, shallow seas where there is enough light for them to grow.

How do reefs grow?

Corals have soft bodies, and grow hard **skeletons** to protect themselves. Corals grow in many different shapes and colours.

fish

This is antler coral. Why do you think it is called this?

antler coral

Coral reefs can take thousands of years to grow.

The Great Barrier Reef off the coast of Australia is thought to have taken about 600 million years to grow!

coral reef

When the old corals die, their skeletons stay on the reef. New corals grow on top of them. Slowly, the reef begins to grow.

Where do reefs grow?

island

coral reef

These coral reefs are around islands in the Indian Ocean.

Most coral reefs grow in the warm, shallow water around islands or along the coast.

Coral reefs mainly grow in tropical seas like the Indian Ocean. Find the Indian Ocean on a world map.

The coral reefs help to protect the coast from high waves and stormy seas.

land

calm water

reef

waves

Waves break on the reef. The water between the reef and the land is calm.

A reef that is close to the land is like a fringe, so it is called a fringing reef.

Barrier reefs

Some coral reefs lie in deeper water and grow in a line along the coast. They are called barrier reefs because they make a barrier between the land and the sea.

Great Barrier Reef

The Great Barrier Reef off Australia is as high as a 40-storey building.

reef

lagoon

island

The waters in a lagoon are calmer than the waters of an open sea.

The sea-water between the reef and the shore is called a **lagoon**. It is protected from the wind and waves of the sea.

A coral island

Many islands are the **peaks** of **volcanoes** under the sea. Sometimes a volcano sinks down below the waves because of movements deep inside the Earth.

This island is the top of a volcano. A coral reef has grown all around it.

coral reef

There was once an island in the middle of this ring of coral. But now it has sunk below the waves and disappeared.

ring of coral

lagoon

The coral reef that once grew around the island remains as a ring of rocks.

A ring-shaped coral island like this is called an atoll.

Rainforests of the sea

Coral reefs are often called the rainforests of the sea because so many different things live there.

fish

coral

A coral reef is crowded and full of life.

coral reef

grey shark

Grey sharks hunt the animals that live on a coral reef.

fish

Small animals live on the reef, feeding on smaller animals or plants. Larger animals visit the reef to find food.

15

Reefs in danger

rough seas

Rough seas batter and break
a coral reef.

coral reef

Coral reefs are hard and stony, but they are still
easy to break. They crack during storms when
the sea pounds them.

The crown-of-thorns starfish feeds on coral. In one day a crown-of-thorns starfish eats enough coral to cover a small table. This much coral can take 100 years to grow.

crown-of-thorns starfish

coral

The crown-of-thorns starfish can be a danger to a reef.

This type of starfish has destroyed large areas of the Great Barrier Reef.

Human damage

diver

coral

This diver is collecting pieces of coral to sell later.

People also damage coral reefs. **Corals** die when divers stand on a reef, knock it with an **anchor**, or break off bits to sell.

People cause **pollution**, which also destroys coral reefs.

Hunters catch the animals and fish that live in coral reefs and sell them. Some of the fish are now very rare because they have been hunted too much.

tropical fish

fisherman

This fisherman has caught a tropical fish to sell as a pet.

The fish that live on coral reefs are often brightly coloured. Look at page 14 to see how brightly coloured they can be.

Saving the reefs

Coral reefs need to be protected. Some are turned into underwater **Marine Parks**. They are **protected by law**.

DO NOT STAND ON ANY CORAL
It is a fragile animal form, easily killed

coral

This coral reef in the US Virgin Islands is now a Marine Park.

breathing mask

These people are learning to dive so that they can visit a coral reef.

People visit the reefs and see the animals and plants that live there. They learn how to protect the reefs.

Special glass-bottomed boats take visitors around coral reefs. People can look at the reef and brightly coloured fish through the glass at the bottom of the boat.

Reef map 1

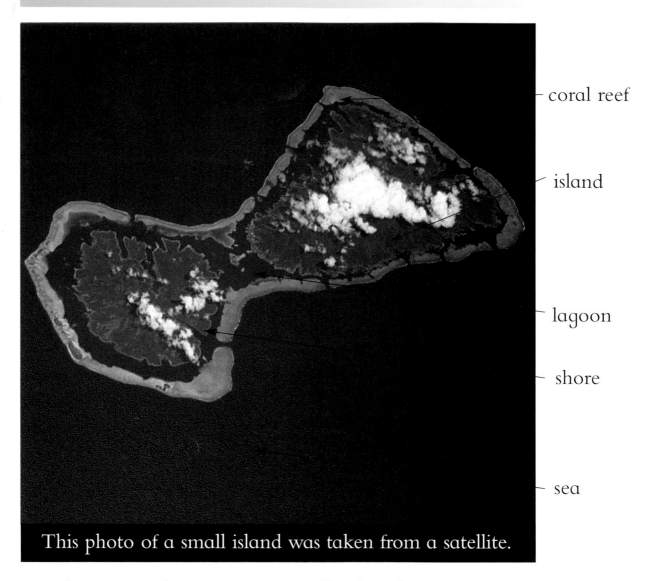

coral reef

island

lagoon

shore

sea

This photo of a small island was taken from a satellite.

This is a photo of a small island. It was taken from a **satellite**. Coral reefs have grown all round the island. There are **lagoons** between the reefs and the shore.

22

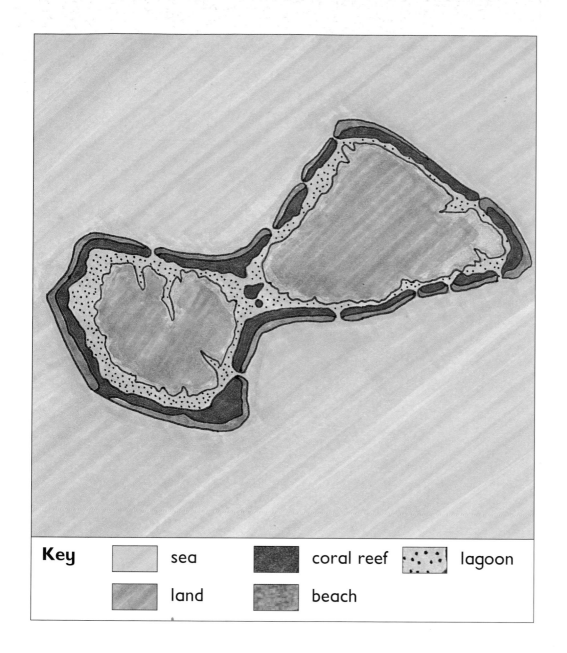

Key

	sea		coral reef		lagoon	
	land		beach			

Maps are pictures of the land. This map shows us the same place as the photo. Use the key to find the coral reefs and the beaches.

Reef map 2

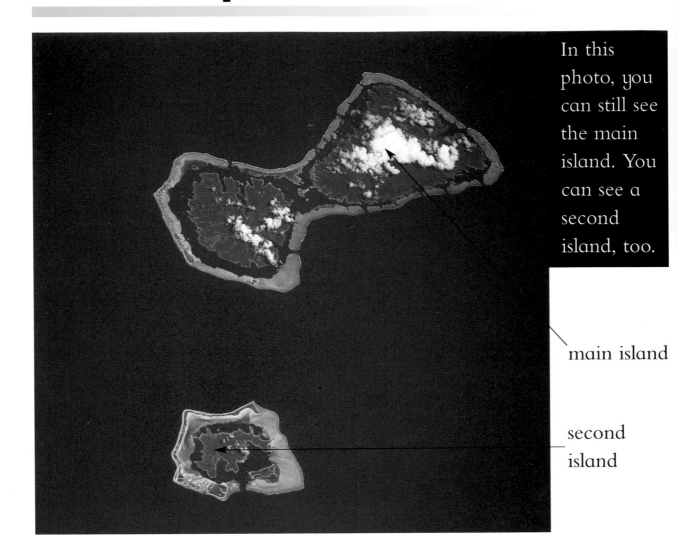

In this photo, you can still see the main island. You can see a second island, too.

main island

second island

This photo shows the same island. The island looks smaller but you can see more of the sea around it. You can see a second island. It has coral around it, too.

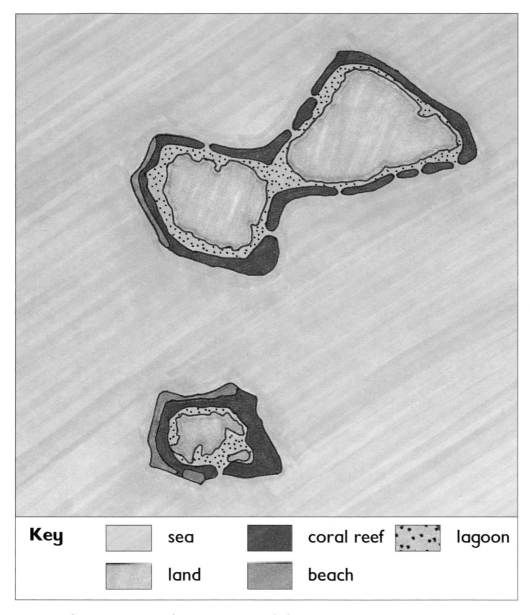

Key		sea		coral reef		lagoon
		land		beach		

On the map the sea is blue. You can see the **lagoon** between the coral reef and the land. The water in the lagoon is shallow and sheltered.

Reef map 3

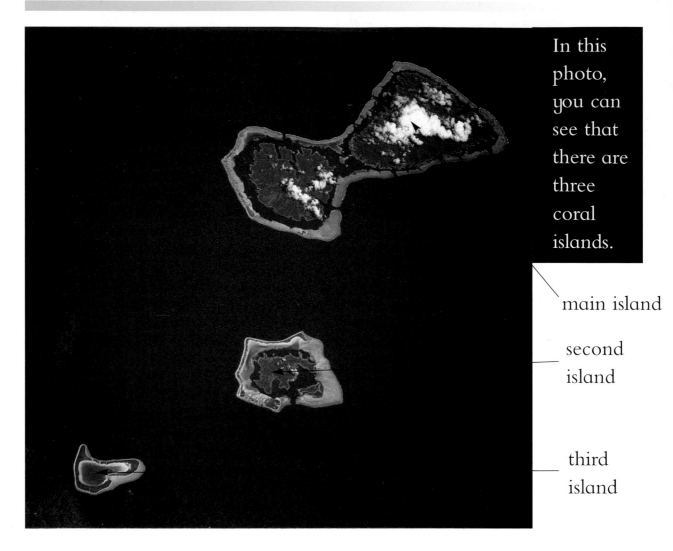

In this photo, you can see that there are three coral islands.

main island

second island

third island

In this photo the islands look even smaller. Now you can see a third coral island nearby. This third island is only made of a coral reef ring. The islands look like big dots in the sea.

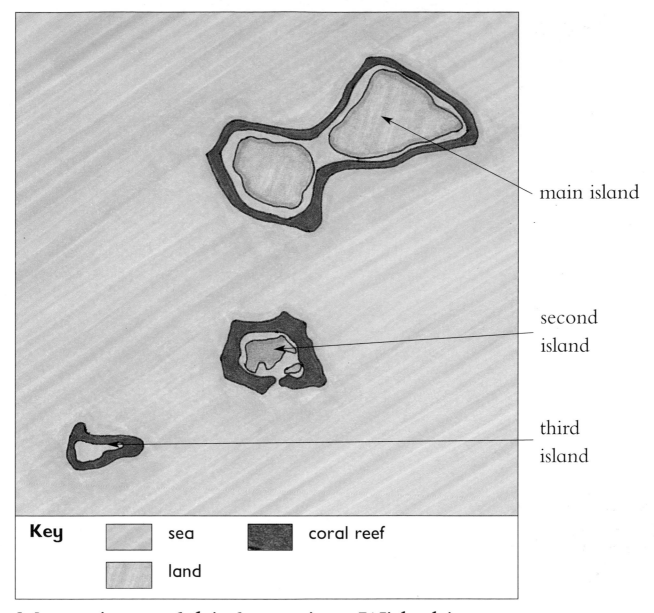

main island

second island

third island

Key | sea | coral reef
| land |

Maps give useful information. With this map it is easy to see which parts of the islands are land and which parts are coral reef.

Amazing reef facts

The Great Barrier Reef is a long line of reefs off the coast of Australia. Altogether, it covers more area than the whole of the United Kingdom.

The Great Barrier Reef is 2027 km long!

shallow water

deep water

brain coral

This wrinkly coral is called brain coral. Why do you think it is called this?

This coral reef is growing in Florida, USA. Florida is cooler than most places where **corals** grow, but the sea here is warm because it flows up from the hotter parts of the world.

Glossary

a b c d e f g h i j k l m n o p q r s t u v w x y z

anchor   a tool that holds a ship in one place. It catches in the sea-bed.

corals   tiny animals that live in the sea. Their skeletons build coral reefs.

lagoon   sheltered water that lies between a barrier reef and the shore

Marine Park   underwater place protected by law to keep it safe and beautiful

peak   very top of a mountain

pollution   when seas are polluted, it means that people have made them dirty and dangerous for wild life

protected by law   there are rules to make sure they are not harmed

satellite   a special machine which goes around the Earth in space. It can take photographs of the Earth.

skeleton   hard part of an animal's body that protects it and gives it its shape

volcano   mountain made out of lava. It sometimes erupts, shooting out hot rock and ash from inside the Earth. Some volcanoes are on the sea-bed.

More books to read

Carole Telford and Rod Theodorou.

Amazing Journeys: Inside a Coral Reef.

Heinemann, 1997

Nicola Baxter.

Our Wonderful Earth.

Two-Can, 1997

Claire Llewellyn.

What Are... Islands?

Heinemann Library, 2001

F. Brooks and K. Khanduri.

First Encyclopedia of Our World.

Usborne, 1999

Index